simply sushi

simply sushi

easy recipes for making delicious sushi rolls at home

Fiona Smith
with photography by Diana Miller

RYLAND
PETERS
& SMALL
LONDON NEW YORK

Designer Vicky Barclay
Senior editor Clare Double
Picture research Emily Westlake
Production Toby Marshall
Art director Leslie Harrington
Publishing director Alison Starling

Notes

All spoon measurements are level unless
otherwise specified.

All eggs are medium unless otherwise specified.
Uncooked or partly cooked eggs should not be
served to the very young, the very old, those
with compromised immune systems, or to
pregnant women.

Ovens should be preheated to the specified
temperature. If using a fan-assisted oven,
cooking times should be reduced according
to the manufacturer's instructions.

Some of the recipes in this book were
previously published in *Easy Sushi Rolls
and Miso Soups*.

All photography by Diana Miller
except the following:
Peter Cassidy Pages 1, 7–15, 18, 34, 54
William Lingwood Pages 4–5, 16
Polly Wreford Page 2

First published in the United States
in 2009 by Ryland Peters & Small
519 Broadway, 5th Floor, New York, NY 10012
www.rylandpeters.com

Text copyright © Fiona Smith and
Ryland Peters & Small 2009
Design and photography copyright
© Ryland Peters & Small 2009

10 9 8 7 6 5 4 3 2 1

Printed and bound in China

Library of Congress Cataloging-in-Publication Data
Smith, Fiona, 1968-
  Simply sushi : easy recipes for making delicious sushi
rolls at home / Fiona Smith ; with photography by Diana
Miller. -- 1st U.S. ed.
    p. cm.
  ISBN 978-1-84597-839-6
1. Cookery (Fish) 2. Sushi. I. Title.
TX747.S5578 2009
641.3'92--dc22
                                         2008040048

contents

the basics

Sushi has come a long way in a relatively short time. It always amazes me to think how the mystique surrounding this style of food kept it from being a favorite with home cooks for so long. Now, however, fresh sushi can be found everywhere from restaurants to supermarkets and fast-food outlets. It is served at elegant parties and home gatherings. Tourists choose sushi restaurants for comforting, familiar food, and children have it in their lunchboxes. Sushi has become this generation's healthy convenience food.

These days, supermarkets sell all kinds of sushi ingredients and utensils. Health food stores are good places to look for seaweed wrappers and Japanese soy sauce, and of course Japanese stores will stock a good range. See over the page and page 12 for more on sushi ingredients.

The traditional techniques used in making sushi can be simplified for the home cook. One of the most popular styles, rolled sushi, is easy and fun to make at home and is the basis of all the recipes in this book. As soon as you have mastered the process of cooking and rolling the rice, you can explore a world of wonderful filling options. There's a step-by-step recipe on page 14 to get you started.

serving sushi

The traditional accompaniments for sushi are soy sauce, wasabi paste, and pickled ginger, and it is often served with miso soup. A smear of wasabi can elevate a piece of sushi from the ordinary to something extraordinary. I have indicated when I think wasabi is important in a recipe. If you do not want to add it in the sushi, serve a small pile on the side, or serve the sushi with a small dish of plain soy and one of wasabi and soy mixed together. Bought wasabi varies immensely; it is possible to find paste with a high percentage of real wasabi, but many are mostly horseradish. See page 63 for more details.

Japanese soy sauce (tamari)

mirin (sweetened Japanese rice wine)

rice vinegar (used for seasoning sushi rice)

Japanese sake or rice wine (see pages 50 and ...)

sheets of nori (dried seaweed used to wrap sushi rolls)

dry gourd (see page 20)

kombu (dried kelp used in cooking sushi rice)

white sesame seeds (see page 30)

black sesame seeds (see page 30)

sliced lotus root (often purchased dried, this has a mild taste and could be used as a topping)

shiso leaf (Japanese herb with a flavor rather like cumin, often used to garnish sushi)

some typical sushi ingredients

fried tofu
(see page 17)

pickled daikon
(see page 17)

fresh ginger root
(used to make
pickled ginger)

short-grain
sushi rice

pickled plums
(see page 58)

pickled ginger
(see page 62)

wasabi paste
(see page 63)

dried shiitake mushrooms
(also available fresh, see page 28)

The key to making sushi is the vinegared rice (*sumeshi*). It has a slightly rounder grain and is stickier than regular long-grain rice, so it holds together better. Never put cooked sushi rice in the fridge—it becomes hard and unpleasant. Instead, keep it covered in a cool place. The vinegar will help to preserve it.

seasoned sushi rice

1¾ cups sushi rice (short grain)

2 inch strip of kombu (dried kelp)

vinegared seasoning

3 tablespoons rice vinegar

4 teaspoons sugar

½ teaspoon salt

makes 4 cups

To make the vinegared seasoning, put the rice vinegar, sugar, and salt in a small bowl and stir until dissolved. (Doing this first gives it time to dissolve.)

Put the rice in a colander and wash thoroughly under cold running water. Leave to drain for 30 minutes (this starts the grains absorbing water).

Put the rice in a medium saucepan, add the kombu, and cover with 1½ cups water. Bring to a boil, stirring, then reduce to a very low simmer. Cover and cook without stirring for 10 minutes. Remove from the heat. Set aside, covered, for 10 minutes.

Transfer the rice to a large, non-metal bowl and remove the kombu. Pour the vinegared seasoning over the rice and, using a wooden spoon, cut the seasoning through the rice, cutting and turning the rice for about 2 minutes. Take care not to mash the grains (you will feel it become stickier as you turn it). Cover the rice with a damp cloth and let cool to room temperature before using.

sushi-making utensils & ingredients

Nori seaweed is the wrapper for your sushi rolls. Choose a brand labeled "ready to use." This means the sheets have been toasted (if not, toast the nori briefly under the broiler) and you can use them straight out of the package. Buy the best grade you can find. You may also see other varieties such as kombu and wakame on sale. Some of the recipes in this book call for half a sheet of nori. When this is so, cut the sheets in half from the shortest side, so you are left with the most width.

There's no substitute for authentic **Japanese sushi rice**—see page 11 for how to cook it.

Japanese soy sauce or tamari is traditionally made without wheat and is more intense in flavor than regular soy sauce.

A bamboo **rolling mat** is inexpensive and can be bought at a large supermarket. You can often use plastic wrap or a clean dishtowel instead; this is indicated in the recipes.

A **Japanese omelet pan** is rectangular, so the omelet is the right shape for rolling and cutting, but you can always use an ordinary round pan.

Wet or dry hands? When making sushi rolls remember that the rice (which can be very sticky) is easier to handle with wet hands, while nori is better handled with dry. The Japanese use "hand vinegar" to make the rice easier to handle. Just pour some water into a bowl and add a splash of vinegar. Keep the bowl and a towel on hand to make the job easier.

Try this simple cucumber roll to start—you will quickly get the hang of the technique and the cucumber filling is easy to handle.

step-by-step cucumber sushi roll

1 sheet of nori

½ recipe seasoned sushi rice (page 11)

½ teaspoon wasabi paste

1 mini cucumber, seeded and sliced lengthwise

to serve

Japanese soy sauce

pickled ginger

wasabi paste

makes 12

1 Cut the nori in half. Put one piece on a rolling mat (rough side up), a piece of plastic wrap, or a dishtowel. Divide the rice in half and press each portion into a cylinder shape. Place one portion on the nori as shown.

2 With the long edge of the nori towards you, spread the rice over the nori, leaving 1 inch nori bare at the far edge. Spread ¼ teaspoon wasabi paste down the center of the rice.

3 Put a cucumber strip on top of the wasabi.

4 Lift the edge of the mat closest to you and carefully roll up the sushi away from you, pressing the ingredients into the roll as you go.

5 You may need to wet the bare edge of nori to seal. Repeat with the remaining nori. Sushi is traditionally served immediately, but if you have to keep it for a while, wrap the uncut rolls in plastic wrap now. Leave in a cool place (not the refrigerator) until you are ready to cut and serve.

6 Use a clean, wet knife (make sure it is sharp) to help you slice into rolls with a neat edge. (You might like to leave a "cockade" of cucumber sticking out from the end of the roll.) Serve with Japanese soy sauce, pink pickled ginger, and wasabi paste.

sushi allsorts
fillings and toppings

Small sushi rolls make great party food, so when you've tried using sushi rice and perhaps made the basic Cucumber Sushi Roll on page 14, try experimenting with different fillings and toppings. Use your choice of the ingredients on the right and arrange them in a line across the rice 1 inch from the front edge. The roll is made and cut as on pages 14 and 15.

- Scallions, finely sliced lengthwise

- Carrots, finely sliced, then blanched

- Pickled daikon, finely sliced lengthwise

- String beans or snake beans, blanched

- Red and/or yellow bell peppers, halved, seeded and sliced into strips

- Trout or salmon caviar

- Smoked fish, cut into long shreds

- Very fresh fish fillets, sliced and marinated in lime juice or rice vinegar for 30 minutes

- Cooked peeled shrimp, halved lengthwise

- Raw or char-grilled tuna, finely sliced

- 3 eggs, beaten, cooked as a very thin omelet, then finely sliced

- Baby spinach leaves, blanched

- Avocado, finely sliced lengthwise

- Fried tofu, sliced into strips

vegetarian
sushi

½ oz. dry gourd*

2 teaspoons salt, for rubbing

1 cup fish stock

2 teaspoons Japanese soy sauce

2 teaspoons mirin (sweetened Japanese rice wine)

1 teaspoon sugar

3 eggs

a pinch of salt

2 teaspoons peanut oil

1½ cups spinach leaves, washed

3 sheets of nori

½ recipe seasoned sushi rice (page 11)

1 small red bell pepper, halved, seeded, and cut into fine strips

1 carrot, grated

a 20 inch skillet with a lid

makes 24

*Gourd (kampyo or calabash) is sold dried in Japanese shops. It is a common ingredient in rolled sushi.

five-color roll

Fill a bowl with water, add the gourd, rub the salt into the gourd to wash it, then drain and rinse thoroughly. Cover the gourd with fresh water and soak for 1 hour. Drain, put in a saucepan, cover with boiling water, and cook for 5 minutes. Drain, return to the pan, then add the fish stock, 1 teaspoon of the soy sauce, 1 teaspoon of the mirin, and the sugar. Bring to a boil, reduce the heat, and simmer for 5 minutes. Let cool in the liquid, then drain.

Put the eggs in a bowl, add the salt and remaining soy sauce and mirin, and mix well. Heat the oil in the skillet over medium heat. Pour in the eggs, swirling the pan so the mixture covers the base. Cook for 2–3 minutes, gently gathering in the cooked omelet around the edges to let the uncooked egg run onto the hot pan. When the egg is set, take off the heat and fold in the 4 sides, so they meet in the middle and the omelet is now double thickness and square. Remove to a board, leave to cool, then slice into 3 strips.

Wipe out and reheat the pan. Add the still-wet spinach and cover with a lid. Cook for 1½–2 minutes until wilted. Tip into a colander and let cool for a few minutes. Using your hands, squeeze out any liquid from the spinach.

Put 1 nori sheet on a rolling mat, rough side up, and spread with one-third of the rice, leaving 1 inch nori bare at the far edge. Put a strip of omelet in the middle and put one-third of the gourd, spinach, pepper, and carrot lengthwise on top.

Carefully roll up the nori in the mat, pressing the ingredients into the roll as you go. Wet the bare edge of nori and finish rolling to seal. Repeat to make 3 rolls, then cut each one into 8 pieces.

A ribbon of zucchini makes a stunning alternative to nori around a sushi roll. It is easiest to cut the zucchini and beet with a mandoline; if you don't have one, use a good sharp peeler or a sharp knife and a steady hand.

pickled zucchini roll
with beet sashimi

1 cup rice vinegar

⅓ cup sugar

2 tablespoons mirin (sweetened Japanese rice wine)

3 zucchini (green or yellow, or both)

1–2 very small beets or 5–6 baby beets, uncooked

1 teaspoon wasabi paste

1½ tablespoons Japanese mayonnaise*

½ recipe seasoned sushi rice (page 11)

dipping sauce

2 tablespoons mild Japanese soy sauce

1 tablespoon sake

makes 18

*Japanese mayonnaise is made with rice vinegar to complement Japanese ingredients. Look for it in specialized stores or online.

To make the pickling mixture, put the vinegar, sugar, and mirin in a small saucepan and bring to a boil, stirring. Reduce to a simmer and cook for 5 minutes. Remove from the heat and let cool.

Thinly slice the zucchini lengthwise, discarding the first and last couple of pieces (they will be too narrow). Arrange the slices flat in a shallow dish or container and pour the pickling mixture over the top. Set aside for 4 hours or overnight.

When ready to assemble the sushi, peel the raw beets and slice as thinly as possible.

Put the wasabi and mayonnaise in a small bowl and mix well.

Divide the seasoned rice into 18 portions about the size of a walnut, and shape each piece into a flattened ball. Wrap a ribbon of pickled zucchini around the outside of each piece, then top with a dab of wasabi mayonnaise and a couple of thin slivers of raw beet.

To make the dipping sauce, mix the soy sauce and sake together and serve in a small bowl beside the sushi.

miso-marinated asparagus roll

24 small or 12 medium
asparagus spears

3 oz. white miso paste

2 teaspoons mirin (sweetened
Japanese rice wine)

1 teaspoon wasabi paste

3 sheets of nori, halved

½ recipe seasoned sushi rice
(page 11)

makes 36

Snap off and discard any tough asparagus ends. Bring a large saucepan of water to a boil, add the asparagus, and simmer for 3–4 minutes until tender. Drain, rinse in plenty of cold water, then let cool. If using medium asparagus, slice each piece in half lengthwise to give 24 pieces. Arrange all the asparagus in a shallow dish.

Put the white miso paste, mirin, and wasabi paste in a small bowl and mix well. Spread evenly over the asparagus and marinate for 2–4 hours.

When ready to assemble the rolls, carefully scrape the marinade off the asparagus—it should be fairly clean, so the miso doesn't overwhelm the flavor.

Put 1 half-sheet of nori, rough side up, on a rolling mat, a piece of plastic wrap, or a dishtowel, with the long edge towards you. Divide the rice into 6 portions. Spread 1 portion in a thin layer on the nori, leaving ¾ inch bare on the far edge.

Put 4 pieces of the asparagus in a line along the middle of the rice. Lift the edge of the mat closest to you and start rolling up the sushi away from you, pressing in the filling with your fingers as you roll. You may need a little water along the far edge to seal it. Repeat to make 6 rolls.

Using a clean, wet knife, slice each roll into 6 even pieces and serve.

Rolling inside-out sushi may seem a bit tricky, but it is actually very easy, because the rice on the outside molds into shape so well. It has the added bonus of looking spectacular.

inside-out avocado roll
with chives and cashews

2 small or 1 large ripe avocado

2 teaspoons freshly squeezed lemon juice

2 tablespoons Japanese mayonnaise (see page 23)

¼ teaspoon salt

1 teaspoon wasabi paste (optional)

3 oz. cashew nuts, pan-toasted (roasted salted cashews also work well)

a small bunch of chives

2 sheets of nori, halved

½ recipe seasoned sushi rice (page 11)

makes 24

Peel the avocado and cut the flesh into small chunks. Toss in a bowl with the lemon juice, mayonnaise, salt, and wasabi, if using. Mash slightly, but not until mushy. Divide into 4 portions.

Chop the cashews and chives very finely and mix in a bowl. Divide into 4 portions.

Put a sheet of plastic wrap on a rolling mat. Put ½ sheet of nori on top, rough side up, with the long edge facing you. Divide the rice into 4 portions and spread 1 portion over the nori.

Sprinkle 1 portion of the nut and chive mixture on top of the rice. Press it in gently with your fingers.

Carefully lift the whole thing up and flip it over so the rice is face down on the plastic wrap. Remove the sushi mat. Put 1 portion avocado in a line along the long edge of the nori closest to you. Roll it up, cut in half, then cut each half into 3, giving 6 pieces. Repeat to make 4 rolls, giving 24 pieces.

mushroom omelet roll

4 oz. fresh shiitake
mushrooms, about 12,
stalks removed

4 oz. oyster mushrooms

2 oz. enoki mushrooms, roots
trimmed (if unavailable, use
oyster and button mushrooms)

3 teaspoons peanut oil

1 tablespoon Japanese
soy sauce

1 tablespoon mirin
(sweetened Japanese
rice wine)

2 eggs

¼ teaspoon salt

½ recipe seasoned sushi rice
(page 11)

4 sheets of nori

a Japanese omelet
pan or 10 inch skillet,
preferably nonstick

makes 24-32

Slice the shiitake and oyster mushrooms into ½ inch slices. Separate the enoki mushrooms into bunches of two or three.

Heat 2 teaspoons of the oil in a large skillet and sauté the shiitake and oyster mushrooms for 2 minutes. Add the enoki and stir-fry for 1½ minutes. Add the soy sauce and mirin and toss to coat. Remove from the heat and let cool. Divide into 4 portions.

Put the eggs and salt in a bowl and beat well. Heat ½ teaspoon of the oil in the omelet pan or skillet. Slowly pour in half of the egg, tipping the pan to get an even coating. Cook for about 1 minute until set, roll up, remove from the pan, and let cool. Repeat with the remaining egg to make a second omelet. Slice the two rolled omelets in half lengthwise.

Divide the rice into 4 portions. Put 1 nori sheet on a rolling mat, rough side up, and spread with 1 portion of rice, leaving 1 inch of bare nori at the far edge. Put a strip of omelet down the middle and top with 1 portion of the mushrooms. Carefully roll up the nori in the mat, pressing the ingredients into the roll as you go. Wet the bare edge of nori and finish rolling to seal. Repeat to make 4 rolls.

Slice each roll into 6-8 pieces and serve.

6 oz. silken tofu

2 tablespoons Japanese soy sauce

1 tablespoon mirin (sweetened Japanese rice wine)

1 teaspoon sugar

3 sheets of nori, halved (you need 5 pieces, so you will have ½ sheet left over)

1 tablespoon white sesame seeds, toasted in a dry skillet

1 tablespoon black sesame seeds

1 tablespoon oboro*

½ recipe seasoned sushi rice (page 11)

1 teaspoon wasabi paste, plus extra to serve

a metal tray, lined with parchment paper

makes 24–32

*Oboro are fine fish flakes, usually colored pink, making them perfect for adding a splash of color to sushi.

broiled tofu roll

To make the silken tofu a little firmer, put it in a bowl and cover it with boiling water before you start making the sushi.

Cut the tofu into ½ inch square strips and arrange in a shallow dish. Put the soy sauce, mirin, and sugar in a small bowl or pitcher and mix well. Pour the mixture evenly over the tofu and marinate for 10 minutes.

Preheat the broiler. Put the tofu on a metal tray lined with parchment paper and broil for 2 minutes, turn the pieces over, brush with marinade, and broil for a further 2 minutes. Set aside to cool.

Cut a half sheet of nori into tiny shreds (about ⅟₁₆ inch), put in a small bowl and stir in the white and black sesame seeds and oboro.

Divide the rice into 4 portions. Spread a sheet of plastic wrap on top of a rolling mat. Put ½ sheet of nori on this and spread with 1 portion of rice. Sprinkle with one-quarter of the seed mixture, then press it lightly into the rice.

Carefully lift the whole thing up and flip it over so the rice is face down on the plastic wrap. Arrange strips of broiled tofu along the long edge of the nori closest to you, smear with a little wasabi paste, and carefully roll up. Repeat to make 4 rolls, then slice each roll into 6–8 pieces.

Serve with extra wasabi and your choice of accompaniments.

This simple little roll makes a colorful addition to a sushi plate. Try using a selection of different vegetables such as carrot, cucumber, radish, beet, and red, yellow, or orange bell peppers.

bright vegetable and thin omelet roll

3 extra-large eggs

2 teaspoons Japanese soy sauce

2–3 teaspoons peanut oil

½ recipe seasoned sushi rice (page 11)

3 sheets of nori, halved

4 oz. mixed vegetables (see introduction), very finely sliced

1 teaspoon wasabi paste (optional)

a Japanese omelet pan or 8 inch skillet

makes 36

Put the eggs and soy sauce in a small pitcher or bowl and beat well. Heat a film of oil in the omelet pan and pour in one-third of the beaten egg mixture. Swirl the egg around to cover the base of the pan and cook for about 1 minute until set. Carefully remove the omelet to a plate and cook the remaining egg mixture in 2 batches. Cut each omelet in half.

Divide the rice into 6 portions.

Put a piece of nori on a rolling mat with the long edge towards you, rough side up. Top with 1 portion of the rice and 1 piece of omelet (trim the end of the omelet if it hangs over the end of the rice). Arrange a line of vegetables along the edge closest to you and smear a little wasabi, if using, in a line next to the vegetables.

Carefully roll up, brushing a little water along the edge of the nori to seal if necessary. Repeat to make 6 rolls, then slice each roll into 6 pieces.

fish & seafood
sushi

Battleship sushi is individually hand rolled so the nori comes about a quarter inch above the rice, leaving room for less manageable toppings such as fish roe. Small cubes of different-colored fish look lovely, and you don't need to be an expert fish slicer to get tender pieces. You do, however, need very fresh raw fish—that is what "sushi- or sashimi-grade" means. Go to a fish market or other outlet where you can be sure the fish is ultra-fresh.

treasures of the sea
battleship sushi

3 oz. piece of sushi-grade raw salmon

3 oz. piece of sushi-grade raw tuna

3 oz. piece of sushi-grade raw white fish (try sea bass, turbot, or halibut)

½ recipe seasoned sushi rice (page 11)

4 sheets of nori

1 teaspoon wasabi paste (optional)

1 tablespoon salmon caviar (keta)

makes 18

Cut the salmon, tuna, and white fish into ¼ inch cubes, put in a bowl and mix gently.

Divide the seasoned sushi rice into 18 portions, a little smaller than a table tennis ball. Gently squeeze each piece into a flattened oval shape, about 1 inch high.

With dry hands, cut the nori sheets into 1 inch strips, and wrap each piece of rice in one strip with the rough side of the nori facing inwards. Seal the ends with a dab of water. You should have about ¼ inch of nori above the rice.

Put a dab of wasabi, if using, on top of the rice, then add a heaped teaspoon of the fish cubes, and a little salmon caviar.

This larger hand roll is still small enough to be held and eaten easily, but also makes a great appetizer or lunch if you allow 3 rolls per person. Choose any smoked fish, but make sure it is moist and soft.

smoked fish hand roll

1 small red onion, finely sliced

1 tablespoon rice vinegar

7 oz. smoked fish, such as trout, salmon, or eel

2 inch piece of cucumber

6 sheets of nori, about 9 x 7 inches

½ recipe seasoned sushi rice (page 11)

1 teaspoon wasabi paste (optional)

1 small carrot, finely sliced into thin strips

1 small red bell pepper, finely sliced into thin strips

makes 18

Put the onion in a small saucepan with the vinegar and ¼ cup water. Bring to a boil, drain, and let cool.

Cut the smoked fish into strips about 2 x ½ inch—you should have 18 even pieces.

Quarter the cucumber lengthwise, scrape out the seeds, then cut into fine strips using a mandoline or vegetable peeler.

Cut each sheet of nori into 3 pieces (3 x 7 inches). Put a piece of nori on a work surface with the long edge towards you and the rough side up. Spread 1 small, heaping teaspoon of rice crosswise over the nori about one-quarter of the way in from the left edge. Smear with a little wasabi, if using. Top the rice with a piece of fish, a few strips of carrot, red pepper and cucumber, and a little red onion.

Take the bottom left corner of the nori and fold it diagonally so the left edge meets the top edge. Continue folding the whole triangle. Arrange with the join downwards on a serving plate or tray. Repeat to make 18 rolls.

These tiny hand rolls are very easy to eat with your fingers, and so make perfect party food, especially when sprinkled with colorful oboro flakes. Mix all the ingredients before rolling the sushi to make the process easier.

california roll

3 inch piece of cucumber

6 oz. crabmeat, fresh or canned

1 small or ½ medium (firm) avocado, cut into small cubes

½ recipe seasoned sushi rice (page 11)

6–7 sheets of nori

1 teaspoon wasabi paste (optional)

1 tablespoon oboro (optional, see page 31)

makes 60–70

Slice the cucumber in half lengthwise and scrape out the seeds. Chop the flesh into tiny cubes and put in a bowl. Add the crabmeat, avocado, and rice and mix gently.

Cut each sheet of nori in half lengthwise, then cut the halves into 5 pieces crosswise (4 x 1½ inches).

Put 1 piece of nori on a work surface with the long edge towards you and the rough side up. Spread 1 teaspoon of the rice mixture crosswise over the nori about one-quarter of the way in from the left edge. Smear the rice with a little wasabi, if using. Take the bottom left corner of the nori and fold it diagonally so the left edge meets the top edge, then continue folding the whole triangle. Sprinkle the open end with a little oboro, if using. Repeat until all the ingredients have been used.

The crunch of tempura batter is delicious in sushi, although the batter will soften as it cools. If you have leftover batter, use it to cook a few vegetables.

tempura shrimp roll

24 large uncooked shrimp, peeled, but with tail fins intact

2 sheets of nori

½ recipe seasoned sushi rice (page 11)

1 teaspoon wasabi paste (optional)

1 cup mizuna or baby spinach

peanut or sunflower oil, for frying

tempura batter

1 egg, separated

1 tablespoon freshly squeezed lemon juice

⅔ cup ice water

scant ⅓ cup all-purpose flour

24 bamboo skewers

makes 24

Thread each shrimp onto a skewer to straighten it for cooking.

To make the batter, put the egg yolk, lemon juice, and ice water in a bowl and whisk gently. Whisk in the flour to form a smooth batter. Do not overmix. Whisk the egg white in a second bowl until stiff but not dry, then fold into the batter.

Fill a large wok or saucepan one-third full of oil and heat to 375°F, or until a small cube of bread turns golden in 30 seconds.

Dip each shrimp in the batter and fry for 1–2 minutes until crisp and golden. Drain on crumpled paper towels and let cool for 5 minutes. Remove the skewers.

With dry hands, cut the nori sheets in half crosswise and then into 1 inch strips. Spread 1 tablespoon rice over each piece of nori, top with a tempura shrimp, a dab of wasabi, if using, and a little mizuna. Roll up to secure the filling. Brush the nori with water to help it stick, if necessary. Repeat until all the ingredients have been used.

Squid is delicious in sushi, but can be tricky when raw, because it does tend to be tough. If you braise it slowly, you end up with deliciously tender pieces.

slow-cooked squid parcels

8 oz. baby squid tubes, 3 inches long (about 12), cleaned

1 teaspoon mirin (sweetened Japanese rice wine)

1 teaspoon Japanese soy sauce

½ teaspoon finely chopped fresh red chile

½ teaspoon finely chopped garlic

1 teaspoon grated fresh ginger

1 tablespoon finely chopped cilantro

½ recipe seasoned sushi rice (page 11)

1 tablespoon black sesame seeds

a baking sheet with sides or broiler pan

makes 24

Preheat the broiler to medium.

Slice the squid bodies in half lengthwise and arrange on a baking sheet or broiler pan. Sprinkle with the mirin and soy. Set the tray at least 6 inches away from the preheated broiler so the heat is not too fierce. Grill for about 8 minutes or until the squid turns opaque. Remove and let cool.

Put the squid in a bowl, add the chile, garlic, ginger, and cilantro, stir gently, cover, and marinate in the refrigerator for 1 hour.

Divide the rice into 24 balls about the size of a small walnut. Top each rice ball with a piece of squid, using the natural curl of the squid body to hold it securely. Sprinkle each with a few black sesame seeds, then serve.

To many sushi fans, delicious raw fish is part of the pleasure of this dish. However, if you're not a fan of uncooked fish, using smoked or pickled fish is a delicious compromise. It is very easy to pickle fish at home, and you can control the sharpness more easily.

pickled salmon roll

3 sheets of nori, halved

½ recipe seasoned sushi rice (page 11), divided into 6 portions

1 teaspoon wasabi paste (optional)

pickled salmon

½ cup rice wine vinegar

2 teaspoons salt

2 tablespoons sugar

finely grated zest of 1 unwaxed lemon

10 oz. salmon fillet, skinned and boned

4 shallots, finely sliced

makes 36–42

To prepare the salmon, put the vinegar, salt, sugar, and lemon zest in a saucepan with ¼ cup water. Bring to a boil, reduce the heat, then simmer for 3 minutes. Let cool.

Put the salmon fillet in a plastic container with the shallots. Pour the vinegar mixture over the top and cover tightly. Refrigerate for 2–3 days, turning the salmon in the pickle once a day.

When you are ready to make the sushi, drain the salmon and shallots. Slice the salmon as finely as possible and divide into 6 portions.

Put a half sheet of nori, rough side up, on a rolling mat, piece of plastic wrap, or a dishtowel, with the long edge towards you. Top with 1 portion of the sushi rice and spread it out in a thin layer, leaving about ¾ inch of bare nori at the far edge. Smear a little wasabi down the center of the rice, if using. Arrange 1 portion of the salmon slices along the middle of the rice and top with a line of the pickled shallots.

Lift the edge of the mat closest to you and start rolling the sushi away from you, pressing in the filling as you roll. You may need a little water along the far edge to seal it. Repeat with the remaining ingredients to make 6 rolls. Using a clean, wet knife, slice each roll into 6–7 even pieces, then serve.

A fresh uncooked oyster makes an elegantly simple topping for sushi. Choose small oysters if possible—large ones will swamp a delicate roll.

fresh oyster roll
with chile cucumber

2 sheets of nori

½ recipe seasoned sushi rice (page 11)

freshly squeezed juice of 1 lemon

20 fresh small oysters, shucked

chile cucumber

½ cup white rice vinegar

2 tablespoons sugar

1 tablespoon mirin (sweetened Japanese rice wine)

3 inch piece of cucumber, halved, seeded, and cut into fine matchsticks

2 mild red chiles, halved, seeded, and finely sliced

makes 20

To make the chile cucumber, put the vinegar, sugar, and mirin in a small saucepan and bring to a boil, stirring. Reduce the heat and simmer for 3 minutes. Remove from the heat and let cool.

Put the cucumber and chiles in a plastic bowl and pour the cooled vinegar mixture over. Cover and refrigerate for 24 hours.

When ready to assemble the rolls, put a sheet of nori, rough side up, on a rolling mat, a piece of plastic wrap, or a dishtowel, with the long edge towards you. Add half the sushi rice and spread it out in a thin layer, leaving about ¾ inch of bare nori on the far edge. Lift the edge of the mat closest to you and start rolling the sushi away from you. You may need a little water along the far edge to seal it. Press the roll into an oval. Repeat with the remaining ingredients to make a second roll. Using a clean, wet knife, slice each roll in half, then each half into 5 even pieces, making 20 in all.

Sprinkle lemon juice over the oysters. Top each sushi roll with an oyster and a little chile cucumber.

Fresh tuna is one of the most popular fillings for sushi. There are three main cuts of tuna, the pink otoro (the finest), chutoro, and the dark red akami. With their incredible popularity and high price tags, otoro and chutoro are delicacies reserved for sashimi, but the akami is perfect for rolled sushi.

spicy tuna roll

10 oz. fresh tuna

2 tablespoons Japanese soy sauce

1 tablespoon sake

1 teaspoon Chinese hot pepper sauce or chile sauce

2 scallions, finely chopped

3 sheets of nori, halved

½ recipe seasoned sushi rice (page 11), divided into 6 portions

makes 36–42

Slice the tuna into ½ inch strips and put in a shallow dish. Mix the soy sauce, sake, hot pepper sauce, and scallions in a bowl. Pour the mixture over the tuna and stir well to coat. Cover and marinate for 30 minutes. Divide into 6 portions.

Put ½ sheet of nori, rough side up, on a rolling mat, with the long edge towards you. Top with 1 portion of the sushi rice and spread in a thin layer, leaving about ¾ inch of bare nori on the far edge. Set one portion of the tuna strips in a line along the middle of the rice.

Lift the edge of the mat closest to you and start rolling up the sushi away from you, pressing in the filling with your fingers as you roll. You may need a little water along the far edge to seal it. Repeat to make 6 rolls. Using a clean, wet knife, slice each roll into 6–7 even pieces.

This is a very Western idea of sushi, but I have it on good authority that it is acceptable. It is also convenient because it uses canned tuna. If you can't find Japanese mayonnaise, good-quality bought mayonnaise works well.

wasabi mayonnaise and tuna roll

6 oz. canned albacore tuna in water, drained

4 teaspoons Japanese mayonnaise (see page 23) or other mayonnaise

1 teaspoon wasabi paste, or to taste

4 oz. baby corn, fresh or frozen, or equivalent drained canned baby corn

4 sheets of nori, with a 1 inch strip trimmed from one long edge of each sheet (reserve these for another use)

½ recipe seasoned sushi rice (page 11), divided into 4 portions

makes 24–28

Combine the tuna and mayonnaise in a bowl and stir in the wasabi.

If using fresh or frozen corn, bring a saucepan of water to a boil and cook the corn for 3 minutes, or until tender. Drain and rinse under cold water to cool. If using canned corn, drain and rinse.

Set a sheet of nori, rough side up, on a rolling mat, a piece of plastic wrap, or a dishtowel, with the long edge towards you. Top with 1 portion of the sushi rice and spread it in a thin layer, leaving ¾ inch of bare nori on the far edge. Spoon one-quarter of the tuna mixture in a line along the middle of the rice and top with a line of corn, set end to end.

Lift the edge of the mat closest to you and start rolling up the sushi away from you, pressing in the filling with your fingers as you roll. You may need a little water along the far edge to seal it. Repeat to make 4 rolls. Using a clean, wet knife, slice each roll into 6–7 even pieces.

meat & poultry sushi

14 oz. boneless, skinless chicken thigh or breast (2 breasts or 4 thighs), cut into ½ inch strips

4 sheets of nori

½ recipe seasoned sushi rice (page 11), divided into 4 portions

1 teaspoon wasabi paste

teriyaki sauce
2 tablespoons Japanese soy sauce

2 tablespoons mirin (sweetened Japanese rice wine)

2 tablespoons chicken broth

teriyaki glaze
1 teaspoon sugar

½ teaspoon cornstarch

miso dipping sauce
2 tablespoons white miso paste

1 tablespoon sugar

½ cup sake

1 small egg yolk

12 bamboo skewers, soaked in water for 30 minutes

makes 24–28

teriyaki chicken roll
with miso dipping sauce

To make the teriyaki sauce, mix the soy sauce, mirin, and chicken broth in a small saucepan and bring to a boil. Remove from the heat and let cool. To make the teriyaki glaze, mix the sugar and cornstarch in a small bowl with a little cold water, then stir in 2 tablespoons of the teriyaki sauce. Set aside.

Thread the chicken strips onto the soaked skewers. Brush the chicken skewers with half the teriyaki sauce and marinate for 10 minutes. Preheat a broiler or outdoor grill to very hot. Cook the chicken skewers for 2–3 minutes, turn over, brush with more sauce, then broil for a further 2–3 minutes until cooked. Remove from the heat, pour the teriyaki glaze over, let cool, then unthread. The chicken must be cold before it is wrapped, or its heat will affect the texture of the roll.

Set a sheet of nori, rough side up, on a rolling mat, a piece of plastic wrap, or a dishtowel, with the long edge towards you. Top with 1 portion of the sushi rice, spreading it in a thin layer covering about half of the nori closest to you. Put one-quarter of the chicken in a line along the middle of the rice and smear with a little wasabi.

Lift the edge of the mat closest to you and start rolling the sushi away from you, pressing in the filling with your fingers as you roll. You may need a little water along the far edge to seal it. Repeat with the remaining ingredients to make 4 rolls. Using a clean, wet knife, slice each roll into 6–7 even pieces.

To make the miso dipping sauce, put the miso, sugar, and sake in a small saucepan over medium heat and bring to a simmer. Reduce the heat to low and cook for 3 minutes, stirring constantly to stop it burning. Remove from the heat and quickly stir in the egg yolk. Strain if necessary and let cool before serving with the sushi.

Pickled plums (umeboshi) can be bought in Japanese and Asian supermarkets. They can be very salty and sharp, so you don't need too much. If you do not like the flavor of pickled plums, replace them with pickled ginger.

sushi balls with roast pork and pickled plums

8 oz. pork tenderloin, in one piece

2 tablespoons Japanese soy sauce

1 tablespoon mirin (sweetened Japanese rice wine)

1 teaspoon Chinese hot pepper sauce or chile sauce

½ recipe seasoned sushi rice (page 11)

10 Japanese pickled plums, halved and stoned

a roasting pan

makes 20

Put the pork in a plastic container. Mix the soy, mirin, and hot pepper sauce in a bowl or pitcher, then pour over the pork. Set aside to marinate for 1 hour, turning the pork in the marinade every 15 minutes.

Preheat the oven to 400°F.

Put the pork in a roasting pan and pour the marinade over. Roast in the preheated oven for 15 minutes. Remove from the oven, let cool, then slice thinly—you should get about 20 slices.

Divide the rice into 20 balls. Take a pickled plum half and push it into the center of a rice ball, then mold the rice around it so it is completely hidden. Repeat with the remaining plums and rice. Top each ball with a slice of roast pork.

Beef tataki is very rare marinated beef served in the sashimi style. If you do not like very rare beef, cook the fillet in a preheated oven at 350°F for 10 minutes before returning to the pan to coat with sauce.

marinated beef sushi
beef tataki

2 teaspoons peanut oil

10 oz. beef tenderloin, in one piece

2 tablespoons Japanese soy sauce

2 tablespoons mirin (sweetened Japanese rice wine)

2 tablespoons rice vinegar

½ recipe seasoned sushi rice (page 11)

shredded pickled ginger, to serve (optional)

pickled red cabbage

about ⅛ red cabbage

½ cup brown sugar

½ cup red wine vinegar

makes 18 / 1 cup pickled cabbage

To make the pickled red cabbage, finely slice the cabbage, removing any large core pieces, and chop into 1 inch lengths. Put in a medium saucepan and add the brown sugar, vinegar, and ¼ cup water. Bring to a boil, reduce the heat, and simmer for 30 minutes. Remove from the heat and let cool. Store in a sealed container in the refrigerator for up to 1 week, or in the freezer for 3 months.

Heat the oil in a skillet and sear the beef on all sides until browned. Mix the soy sauce, mirin, and vinegar and pour over the beef, turning the meat to coat. Remove immediately from the heat and transfer the beef and its sauce to a dish. Let cool, cover, and refrigerate for 1 hour, turning once.

Divide the rice into 18 and shape into firm ovals.

Cut the beef in half lengthwise (along the natural separation line), then slice as finely as possible. Wrap a piece of beef over each rice ball and top with a little pickled red cabbage or pickled ginger.

accompaniments

Pickled ginger is the traditional companion of sushi. The subtle flavoring of raw fish, delicate rice, and fresh vegetables can easily be overpowered by the lingering flavors of previous morsels. Ginger helps cleanse the palate, introducing a sharp freshness that stimulates the taste buds for the next delight.

pickled ginger

6 oz. piece of fresh ginger

1 tablespoon salt

½ cup rice vinegar

½ cup plus 1 tablespoon sugar

1 slice fresh beet, 1 red radish, sliced, or a drop of red food coloring (optional)

makes about 1 cup

Peel the ginger and slice it very finely with a mandoline or vegetable peeler. Put it in a large sieve or colander and sprinkle with salt. Set aside for 30 minutes, then rinse thoroughly.

Put the rice vinegar and sugar in a saucepan, add ¼ cup water and bring to a boil, stirring until the sugar has dissolved. Boil for 5 minutes. Let cool, then pour over the ginger. If you would like it to be pink, like store-bought ginger, add the beet, radish, or food coloring. Cover and refrigerate for at least 24 hours or until needed.

wasabi paste

Most of the wasabi we buy in tubes is mixed horseradish and wasabi—or just horseradish, dyed green. Always buy the best available variety. Many Japanese cooks mix their own paste from silver-gray wasabi powder (sold in small cans, like paprika), believing that the flavor is stronger and sharper. The fresh roots are not widely available, even in Japan, but if you see them in a specialty greengrocer (on a bed of ice), do try them to experience the real flavor of wasabi. Wasabi is traditionally grated using a sharkskin grater, but a porcelain ginger grater or very fine zester will also work.

wasabi from powder

1 teaspoon wasabi powder

serves 1

Put the wasabi powder in a small bowl or eggcup. Add 1 teaspoon water and mix with the end of a chopstick. Serve immediately. If you have to wait a few minutes before eating, turn the bowl upside down to stop the air discoloring the wasabi.

wasabi from the fresh root

1 fresh wasabi root

serves 6–8

Scrape or peel off the rough skin from the root. Using a circular motion, rub the wasabi gently against an abrasive grater (such as a ginger grater or zester) onto a chopping board. Pound and chop the grated wasabi to a fine paste with a large knife or cleaver. Consume within 10 minutes; the heat in fresh wasabi lasts only that long.

index

conversion charts
**Weights and measures have been
rounded up or down slightly to
make measuring easier.**

Volume equivalents:

American	Metric	Imperial
1 teaspoon	5 ml	
1 tablespoon	15 ml	
¼ cup	60 ml	2 fl.oz.
⅓ cup	75 ml	2½ fl.oz.
½ cup	125 ml	4 fl.oz.
⅔ cup	150 ml	5 fl.oz. (¼ pint)
¾ cup	175 ml	6 fl.oz.
1 cup	250 ml	8 fl.oz.

Weight equivalents:

Imperial	Metric
2 oz.	50 g
3 oz.	75 g
4 oz.	125 g
6 oz.	175 g
7 oz.	200 g
8 oz. (½ lb.)	250 g
10 oz.	300 g
14 oz.	425 g

Measurements:

Inches	Centimeters
½ inch	1 cm
¾ inch	1.5 cm
1 inch	2.5 cm
2 inches	5 cm
3 inches	7 cm
4 inches	10 cm
7 inches	18 cm
8 inches	20 cm
9 inches	23 cm
10 inches	25 cm

Oven temperatures:

180°C	(350°F)	Gas 4
190°C	(375°F)	Gas 5
200°C	(400°F)	Gas 6